BRISTOL SIX-CYLINDER CARS

CHRISTOPHER BALFOUR

AMBERLEY

First published 2024

Amberley Publishing
The Hill, Stroud,
Gloucestershire, GL5 4EP

www.amberley-books.com

ISBN: 978 1 3981 1974 1 (print)
ISBN: 978 1 3981 1975 8 (ebook)

British Library Cataloguing in Publication Data.
A catalogue record for this book is available from the British Library.

Typeset in 10pt on 13pt Celeste.
Typesetting by SJmagic DESIGN SERVICES, India.
Printed in the UK.

Contents

Foreword

My father, Sir George S. M. White, 3rd Baronet, who was responsible for founding the Car Division of the Bristol Aeroplane Company, preferred to avoid the limelight. He was well known for his sense of humour, his kindness, his concern for his workforce, and above all for his passion for quality, but, like W. O. Bentley, he disliked personal publicity. As a young man he studied engineering at Cambridge University under William (later Sir William) Farren, coming down early to gain practical experience in the Engine Division of the Bristol Aeroplane Company, of which his father was a founder and managing director. He had raced motorboats from his teenage years both with and against the Bristol Aeroplane Company's genius chief engineer Roy Fedden, building a close relationship with Fedden and his staff. As he developed his engineering and racing skills, he came, for a period in the late 1930s, to hold more water speed records than any other individual. He built his first hydroplane himself.

By the start of the Second World War he had become the Bristol Aeroplane Company's works manager, rising to become responsible for its Aircraft Division producing airframes for Blenheims, Beaufighters and all the subsequent derivatives. After the war, he turned his attention to the manufacture of cars. He served as the Bristol Aeroplane Car Division's managing director and chairman for many years, during which the division claimed many international rallying and racing triumphs. He was much involved in all design development until, in 1959, the government-enforced merging of the aircraft industry split the Aeroplane Company, leaving its Car Division without an effective parent. He bought the division largely to protect the future of his loyal and skilled workforce and to continue the production of the finest possible vehicles.

In September 1969 my father's own car was hit by a laundry van in slow-moving traffic, a minor accident that led, by almost unbelievable misfortune, to serious injury. When, in 1973, it became obvious to him that he would never recover sufficiently to return to work, he decided with the greatest reluctance to part with his majority shareholding in Bristol Cars, again to ensure continuity and a future for his employees. The new owner was a charismatic character who deserves credit for keeping the company afloat at times when equally famous automotive names were failing. In old age he came gradually to reinvent the early history of Bristol Cars, often representing himself as the key player in its early development.

Inevitably, as memories of my father's devotion to the marque faded, journalists and the general public came to believe that Bristol Cars had always been the small-time business that it seemed to have become. Its original reputation for advanced engineering to genuine aircraft standards had gradually slipped away.

Since the final collapse of the company and the death of the second owner, two major works have been published, both of which firmly set the record straight. The first, *The Bristol Aeroplane Company's Car Division* compiled by Palawan Press, was published in 2018. The second, *Aero Dynamic – How Bristol Won at Le Mans*, was written by Simon Charlesworth and published by Butterfield Press in 2022. Both strip away layers of misconception that have come to overlay the early history of Bristol Cars and highlight its triumphs. But both are very high-quality limited editions and inevitably priced beyond the means of many motoring enthusiasts.

Christopher Balfour, universally accepted as the leading authority on the development of the Bristol company, now makes this remarkable story available to all. He and his publisher, Amberley Publishing, are to be congratulated for returning to my father and the many skilled craftsmen, designers and engineers who worked with him, the recognition that is rightly theirs. Owners of surviving 2-litre Bristol cars will be delighted too, for they have always appreciated what many had forgotten – the exceptional nature of the machinery they are privileged to drive.

Sir George White

A gathering of six-cylinder cars at Napier, North Island, New Zealand.

1

Junior Partner in Bristol Aeroplane

BAE Systems, partner in Airbus, and today challenger to Boeing, is the legacy of a Bristol enterprise which, if different decisions had been taken, could also have provided cars to fill the spaces now occupied by BMW, Mercedes, Lexus, etc. Over three generations, the White family, their Smith relations and their employees spent their lives on transport endeavours and were responsible for some magnificent achievements. As is the way of human life, they were hindered by events over which they had no control. Fundamental to understanding is the relationship between entrepreneurs and the State, and the interplay between peace and war. Without this family's efforts and dedication there could have been a different outcome to the twentieth century's two world wars.

George White was born in Bristol in 1854. By 1880 he was a member of the Bristol Stock Exchange, specialising in transport shares. He was asked to act as Secretary of Bristol's new horse-drawn tramway service. In the 1890s he saw the potential of new power sources and was the pioneer of an electric tramway running from the middle of the city to the suburb of Kingswood. With another pioneer, Clifton Robinson, tramways were also created in London and other cities. Fifteen years later Bristol trams were augmented by petrol power. When the buses purchased proved inadequate for city gradients, George, by then Sir George, decided to manufacture his own Bristol vehicles. A new factory was built at Filton, north of the city.

In 1910 this Filton factory became the centre for aircraft manufacture. Sir George's son, Stanley White, was appointed Managing Director at Filton in 1911 with his nephew Herbert Thomas becoming Works Manager in January 1912. Bus production, joined by lorries and taxis, reverted to the Tramways site in Brislington with Sir George's younger brother, Samuel, remaining as Managing Director. The future control of an entrepreneur's achievement often leads to difficulties which can be compounded by tax demands. This was the case when Sir George died in 1916. Tax payment and the later unexpected terms of his brother Samuel's will resulted in Sir George's sister's family, the Smiths, jointly having a majority shareholding. Sir George's son, Stanley White, was confirmed as Managing Director with responsibility for all aeroplane manufacture, but he had a smaller shareholding than the Smiths. When Samuel White died in 1928, those unexpected terms in his will left his controlling interest in both companies to

George White talking with Samuel Cody, an American who made the first recorded powered flight in England in 1908.

George White and Maurice Tabuteau with a Bristol T-Type, probably at Hendon before the start of a European race.

the three Smith brothers and their two sisters. Thus it was that William Smith (later Verdon Smith) became chairman with the Smiths arbiters of fundamental decisions. It was William who in the 1930s decided to sell the controlling interest in commercial vehicles to Thomas Tilling. Harold Penrose, personally involved in and knowledgeable about British aviation, recorded in one of his histories, 'The Bristol Aeroplane Company

Stanley White and his son George in Scotland in 1920 with Buick Tourer.

had extended both its engine and aeroplane factories and in 1939 the buildings covered over two million square feet making it the largest single aircraft manufacturing plant in the world.' Whether for patriotic or other reasons, the decision to concentrate on aeroplanes and aero engines, rather than the lorries, was to play a massive part in the country's defence. But, for the record, this Smith-side decision would mean no commercial vehicle back-up, no Mercedes-like ambulances outside all the hospitals if, in the future, the family opted for wheeled as well as winged transport (Mercedes do not make aeroplanes).

By the start of the Second World War the first George's grandson, Stanley's son, another George (G. W.), after studying engineering at Cambridge under W. S. Farren, and, back at Filton, experiencing the shop floor, was working in the factory supervising production. (Farren became Sir William, Director of the Royal Aircraft Establishment at Farnborough.) Churchill had appointed Lord Beaverbrook as Minister for Aircraft Production. G. W. was the kind of person praised by 'The Beaver' in his book *Don't Trust to Luck*: 'Not a touch of arrogance and able to work with others.' G. W. was there that September day in 1940 when ninety-seven German bombers flew over Filton bent on destruction. Ninety-one employees were killed or mortally wounded, 147 were wounded. He was there amongst the unexploded bombs attending to casualties and damaged planes. Together, spurred by the much older 'Beaver', who used to personally talk with G. W., Filton employees went on to produce around 11,000 Beaufighters, Beauforts and Blenheims plus superb aero engines. G. W.'s courage and relations with employees was such that he was supported when car manufacture was considered as a way, if victory was achieved, of providing employment using family resources. Of course, there were some disputes but Filton was not, like the Midlands, a scene of struggle with the unions (legacy of 1930s unemployment) or the banks. The Filton endeavour, with strong financial reserves, would not be three sided, managers,

Stanley White and his son George in Switzerland, 1934.

workers and financiers in conflict as bedevilled established British car companies till the Germans and Japanese took the reins.

G. W. had long appreciated the pleasure that a well-designed car could give to both driver and passengers – he had owned an Aston Martin. He had supported Roy Fedden's ideas about building Alfa Romeos at Filton in the 1930s and had used a 4 ¼-litre Bentley during the war years. He believed there would be a market for a small car of similar quality to the Bentley and that it would be needed quickly after all the destruction. There would be benefit in starting by developing an existing product if anything could be found. This would give the Filton engineers time to develop their own complete Bristol car and advance their own methods of manufacture. He was thinking of a 3-litre, six-cylinder, four-door, five-seater he called a 'World Car' with much better suspension than pre-war designs, able to transport driver and passengers in comfort over poor road surfaces. G. W. believed that Filton employees could provide a standard of workmanship which would compare favourably with any other manufacturer. The attitude this author encountered when working on a Coventry production line in the 1950s – 'don't bother about that fault, get the cars out of the doors, dealer or customer can sort' – was anathema to him. G. W. calculated that costs could be covered with an output of ten cars a week. They would hope to sell double that number after a few years when Bristol was established on the market.

In May 1945, the month the war ended, one Donald Aldington, then working as a Ministry Inspector, visited Eric Storey, one of G. W.'s assistants, at Filton. In conversation Donald mentioned that, with his two brothers, H. J. and W. H., they would like to market a car with the virtues of the four-door saloon BMW 326 which, with the two-door drophead 327 and the two-seater 328, their company, AFN, had imported from Germany before the war. The three Aldington brothers, H. J., W. H. and D. A., spearheaded by the entrepreneurial H. J., had built chain drive Frazer Nash cars in the early 1930s. H. J. had first visited BMW in 1935 when he had driven their 319 in the Kesselberg Hill Climb. This car had been developed from the Dixi, itself a descendent of the British Austin Seven. BMW had taken over Dixi in 1928. These designs shared axle supporting rear springs which were only attached to the car's chassis frame at their front end. BMW's Fritz Feidler replaced the Austin's quarter eliptics by torsion bars with a triangular linkage from either side of the propellor shaft tunnel. The BMW had swiftly become appreciated for this superior rear suspension. Those torsion bars meant that chassis extension to provide attachment points for the rear of the leaf springs was not necessary. The front of the car was less revolutionary. A well-located transverse leaf spring still enabled plenty of independent wheel movement. Together with precise rack and pinion steering, the car which they marketed as the Frazer Nash BMW had an agility unknown to pre-war British drivers.

H. J. Aldington had wanted to encourage the production of a post-war British car with these qualities in one of the Midland factories. In 1945 he went visiting in a 327. There was no response until he got to Standard. Even there, after initial enthusiasm, Sir John Black had then rejected any cooperation. Eric Storey reported what he had learnt about AFN's post-war ambition to G. W. He realised that experience with such a BMW could be what was needed to learn about making cars. G. W. discussed with his cousin Reginald (R. V-S.), a trained lawyer and son of William Verdon-Smith. R. V-S. had been part of the wartime

H. J. Aldington at the start of Kesselberg hill climb. BMW 319, 1935.

Type 326 Rear Axle with Torsion Bar Suspension.

Original BMW rear axle with torsion bar suspension.

Eric Storey with early Beutler-bodied car.

central administration whilst G. W. had become Managing Director of the Aircraft Division in 1943. They had both joined the Board of BAC in December 1942. G. W. and R. V-S. arranged to meet up with H. J. Aldington at Isleworth. Alan Goodyear, a friend of many years and still restoring historic cars today, has told me about his apprenticeship with AFN at that time. This had been arranged by his father, a skilled and experienced pilot who had taught H. J. to fly the Messerschmitt Taifun imported in the late 1930s. Alan remembers H. J. as the epitome of the 'can do' man of action, securing competitive rates for the supply of parts from outside firms, in the workshops helping to solve problems, personal contact with owners and prospective customers, driving cars like TMX 545 at Le Mans in 1949. G. W. and R. V-S. liked the cars they were shown and were also made aware of the four-door, 3.5-litre BMW 335 introduced just before the war. Concern came from the observation that H. J. did not operate like their many other business partners. H. J. did not seem to be the sort of person to write detailed reports for consideration by the mighty Board at Filton.

After discussion over many months and some turbulence over how much H. J. should become involved with work at Filton, it was agreed that Bristol's first effort should be building up a complete car based on the two-door, 2-litre BMW. The reasoning was that such a car's specific market, that is not family transport but rather recreational, would hopefully lead to contact with involved owners. G. W. wanted the four-door car, which would follow in much greater numbers, to be Bristol's own design in every detail. They did not want a copy of the 335. AFN would become one of the main but not the only selling and service agent for the cars. H. J. would receive one of the first saloons for demonstration which he could also drive in rallies. H. J. was also encouraged to develop his existing contacts with European coachbuilders. Bristol would supply completed chassis as requested. They would also build engines for post-war Frazer Nash sports cars. (Alan Goodyear also remembers 100 mph test drives along the old Staines Road in the Le Mans Replicas.)

Whilst these negotiations were taking place, the Aldington brothers re-established their relationship with what remained of BMW. They visited Munich where Fritz Feidler, Rudolf

Design conference at Filton. Dudley Hobbs with glasses and to his left Jan Lowy and Jim Lane. Looking at model of 401 layout.

Fritz Feidler with H. J. Aldington.

Schleicher and others were delighted to see old friends – engineers can share technical knowledge and heritage whatever their political masters get up to. The Aldingtons played a significant part in stopping BMW spoils being taken to America. BMW favoured the Filton plan. It was agreed that Bristol could have BMW drawings and that they could purchase engines and other parts. G. W. carefully checked that there were no patent implications or legal hindrance to manufacture. In these ways Bristol helped BMW get back on their feet after the war.

2

German Legacy: The 400

The Bristol Aeroplane Company was in a strong position in 1945. They answered the government's request to make pre-fabricated houses using light alloy materials and aircraft techniques. They were soon in production with the tough Freighter/Wayfarer 'workhorse of the air'. G. W. had been involved with its conception and was a strong supporter. They were to build 214 examples well remembered for their use as cross-channel ferries. On one occasion back in the 1960s, the author embarking with the 400 at HURN Airport found that the other traveller was driving an almost new 406. Bristol's own proposal to update the American Constellation had been rejected by the politicians for patriotic reasons. Instead they were committed, at the tax-payer's expense, to the giant Brabazon airliner designed to improve on the pre-war form of luxury air travel for the few exemplified by the pre-war 'Empire' flying boats (in which the author flew to India in 1948). The government

Freighter 'workhorse' loading Bristol.

committee charged with looking at post-war aircraft needs had failed to anticipate the future market looking for faster, less luxurious travel.

Despite the Brabazon, there was still a background of a sound financial future for Bristol. G. W.'s relatives and fellow directors accepted his report that there would not be profit from the car project until production of a totally new Bristol-designed 3-litre five-seater planned for the next decade. Meanwhile they would learn how to make cars from the BMW legacy. In September 1945 the government released companies from the ban on private ventures and Bristol were able to start building up the car enterprise. The new car company was established as part of the Light Engineering Division with George Abell as General Manager. A. F. Elliott would take charge of the initial engine and gearbox production at Bristol Engines. E. Mathew (Christian name not recorded) would look after the workshop area in which the prototypes would be put together. Dudley Hobbs forsook aeroplanes to follow his car interest as chief designer. In time he was to be joined by Jan Lowy, Jack Channer, Dennis Sevier and others who will come into the story.

For a short time John Perrett brought AFN knowledge to Filton before he went to other work. The family directors were closely involved in the start-up years. R. V-S., the lawyer, headed negotiations with H. J. and commented on the early cars he drove. He had previously owned a Speed Twenty Alvis. Sir Stanley, the author has been told, greatly enjoyed his cars back to the 1903 10hp Panhard Levassor, which is still with the family today, and a successful Brighton Run entrant. Like G. W. he drove Bentleys during the war. R. V-S.'s father, Sir William, and cousin Herbert Thomas (until his unexpected death after surgery in 1947) also appreciated Bentleys. Herbert owned some magnificent 6.5-litre examples, one at least with body built at Filton.

A 2-litre BMW was taken to pieces with supervision by Eric Storey and Donald Stock. (Donald was later to supervise work at the Chiswick Service Department.) New

Stanley White with Vauxhall 30/98.

components were made with imperial in place of metric measurements. Material quality was upgraded. R. V-S. drove a two-door 327 supplied by AFN. The engine was taken out to be copied by the engine division. Another cylinder block, again from AFN, was sent for examination by Sterling Metals. They decided, for more strength, to incorporate bronze inserts surrounding the holes for the sparking plugs. This is the reason for the small 10-mm plugs. It is just one example of how Filton's creation would have better components. Whilst Roy Fedden was no longer with Bristol, the engine department he had striven to create had long experiences with avoiding metal fatigue. Components were made with smooth surfaces and generous radii. By the end of the year Filton had created a better than BMW engine, though not without fault. Some cylinder heads had to be replaced under warranty. Not all water drained out through the bottom hose, which led to cracking. Also, after many years' service, cracks were found in some early cylinder block sidewalls.

By spring 1946 they had built a prototype chassis. Interviewed many years later, an employee of that time remembered how this body-less creation was driven constantly from Filton to Land's End and back and then, after each trip, up and down the steps of the canteen. Such treatment was possible because of Bristol's own design of rotary front shock absorbers added to the BMW-type transverse leaf. As an improvement on the German design, two clamps were provided for that spring. This allowed the spring leaves to flex between them so that roll on one side was not transmitted to the other side. This flexing

Early chassis. S. U. carburettors.

16

meant a little movement of the centre bolt and occasionally early bolt heads broke off. The response was to add safety links to keep the spring secure then later to use a tapered bolt larger near its head and made of better-quality steel. The kingpin design had an inclination angle which allowed the suspension to lie back at 9 degrees to help absorb shocks. Jack Channer referred to the 400 as a real rough road eater. Journalists from *The Autocar* were mightily impressed when they visited Filton that summer. They commented: 'The car can travel at 30 mph over road surfaces so bad that a normal chassis would shake the occupants badly. Furthermore it's cornering at speed is refreshingly good and the steering as positive as anything that has ever been built.' They did not mention the Enots system of lubrication by oil fed through pipes to each separate suspension joint and the steering rack and pinion. This is 'total loss' operated by a separate pedal above the brake and clutch pedals. The pedal should be pressed every 100 miles. When operating correctly there is a pleasing feel to the steering, but, however carefully maintained, there will be a little dribble through the tiny drainage hole at the bottom of the Wilcot patent oil-resistant gaiters. Owners accept this and travel with a sheet of cardboard if visiting houses with pristine drives.

G. W. was not one for seeking praise but the *Autocar* team signalled progress, which would have provided encouragement. It is fortunate that a copy of G. W.'s mammoth ten-page report giving the state of play in July 1946, and suggesting the way ahead, has become available. It had been agreed that the car company would have its own manufacturing space. This would be segregated from the main factory where the engines and other components would be made. The family directors still supported and accepted the losses. G. W. wrote that they had already provided £200,000 for initial research and development. He believed these premises 'would be sufficient for the time being and capable of expansion in a year or two if we find that the demand for our type of car exists throughout the world in the same numbers as we understand was the case when BMWs were in full swing before the war'. The plan was that the drawing office would start on the expanded chassis of the five-seat, four-door saloon in October with the car 'cleared for production' eighteen months later in March 1948. Production would start with the 2-litre engine in June 1948 whilst the design of the larger engine continued. The 3-litre, five-seat, four-door would follow in June 1949. The report gives further glimpses of their thinking – a potentially massive world market for the right car and the money would come rolling back in. 'Do we have one car in every country in the world or a lot of cars in one or two countries?' And then the percipient vision from this far-thinking man: 'Are we considering licences? Tata of India, one of the largest engineering firms in the world, might start by making bodies with a view to full licence in a year or two.' Brought up with, and immersed in, his family's global achievements, he saw what might be possible if the right decisions were taken. This is the fascination of the story – and now Tata own Jaguar!

A letter to Don Aldington from G. W. confirms that the first complete car was driven to the paint shop on 25 September 1946, seventeen months after Eric Storey's initial 1945 meeting and subsequent discussion with G. W. The first Bristol-built engine had been on the test bed in May. In September (1946) engine No. 5 was fitted to the 327, which R. V-S. had been using. H. J. then took this car, JHX 338, to visit potential coachbuilders in Europe. He drove 2,000 miles including Alpine passes. He reported 'a first-class sports engine, apparently unbreakable and stands flogging unmercifully'. Amongst other matters he mentioned oil leaks and questioned jet sizes, matters which are still relevant to owners.

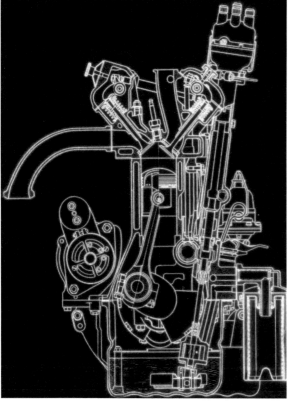

Above: Engine assembly at Filton.

Left: Engine drawing showing cross-over pushrod.

Journalists, this time from *The Motor*, came to Filton at the end of October. With a detailed drawing by Theo Page, the merit of the BMW engine design was explained: 'There is a single chain driven camshaft mounted in the block. Each inlet valve is worked by a pushrod and rocker, but the exhaust valve mechanism is operated by another set of transverse pushrods which carry the motion from the camshaft across the head. The inclined overhead valves and direct down-draught ports are largely responsible for the excellent performance.' At BMW before the war Rudolf Schleicher had achieved more power without moving the camshaft from its position low in the block as in the original design.

Critics of wooden body frames were exemplified by a correspondent from Johannesburg: 'Any-one with experience of South Africa will confirm that the best of wooden bodies will not stand up to extreme and sudden changes of temperature and humidity coupled with rough and corrugated roads.' G. W. responded to critics by explaining that Filton did not yet have facilities for making steel car bodies. What they did have was a woodworking department short of work after the war where their skilled workers would be able to copy the BMW body shape. G. W. also reckoned that the initial customers they were seeking would accept this first car despite the limited rear legroom because of the other attributes. In practice these bodies were so well built that, when they reached Australia, the wood construction stood up well to those equally challenging road conditions. This excellence did not stop discussion about alternatives or future coachwork without the wooden frame. If Filton could not yet provide, what would other coachbuilders create if Bristol sent them chassis? This is where H. J.'s knowledge and contacts organised through AFN were helpful. Factory records recently found confirm that twenty-four chassis were sent to Switzerland between 1947 and 1950. Most were despatched to C. A. Drenowatz, the agent in Switzerland well known to H. J. It seems that these seven cars were bodied as dropheads by Farina in Turin. Then in the AFN archive there is a record of the earlier H. J. and R. V-S. visit to Eng Bianchi Anderloni at Stabilimenti Turinga in Milan in 1946. R. V-S. was so impressed by what he saw, 'a real combination of artists and craftsmen', that Dudley Hobbs had been summoned to join them by train. R. V-S. preferred the body on the Lancia Aprilia chassis to the wider body for the bigger Alfa Romeo. (Dudley's intensive report on this visit is considered in the next chapter.)

Farina drophead back at Filton.

Left: First 400, JHY 261 in Milan. David Murray, Signor Fillipini, Count Lurani and H. J. Aldington.

Below: Reginald Verdon-Smith in JHY 261.

There is uncertainty but probably at least eight 'Superleggera' bodies were built on Bristol chassis forwarded from Switzerland to Milan. Of the remaining, say, eight chassis, three bodies were built by Beutler at Thun, two saloons and one a drophead, one a coupe by Ghia Aigle and one a drophead by Langenthal. There has been suggestion that Langenthal received but did not use another chassis; also a note suggesting one was returned to Filton for scrap. On this reckoning that leaves one chassis unaccounted for. And either Farina or Turinga may have built a further car. In the UK two chassis went to Broughton's of Cheltenham. One was built up as a shooting brake to benefit from the consequent tax concession. It still exists. The other is reckoned to have been made into a drophead for a doctor in Herefordshire. There is no trace of this car at the time of writing. Another chassis was sold to University Motors whose University Coachworks subsidiary were responsible for building up their own drophead. Panelled in steel rather than aluminium, and with electric motors for the windows in the doors, the result was a heavy car.

Back at Filton development continued and a drophead body was built. The saloon and this drophead were then driven to the March 1947 Geneva show by R. V-S. and H. J. George Abell was with them on this trip. R. V-S. subsequently commented 'spare wheel in an impossible position, no room for golf clubs, inadequate cabin blower'. Changes were made. Then came another political cannonball. Purchase tax was to be increased from 33 to 66 per cent for cars costing over £1,000. They decided to concentrate on the saloon,

Unique 400 shooting brake built on new chassis by F. J. Hyde of Hereford.

Saloon and drophead travelling to 1947 Geneva show.

knowing that Farina and other coachbuilders could provide open-top cars. *The Motor* magazine wrote in the first full test in May 1948: 'clings tenaciously to the road, a quite exceptional standard of comfort riding over bad roads. Immense capacity for hard work.' The following January, 1949, Zdenek Treybal achieved third place in the first post-war Monte Carlo Rally. H. J. was second in the touring class of the 1949 Targa Florio in Sicily and third in the touring category of the Mille Miglia.

Left: Zdenek Treybal, third place in the 1948 Monte Carlo Rally.

Below: H. J. Aldington, second place Touring Class, 1949 Targa Florio.

Gordon Greig's 400 in Australia at the 1954 Mount Druitt 24 Hours Road Race.

There is still the clear memory of visiting Filton after our purchase of a 400 over sixty years ago. Eric Storey had been in post as Service Manager for ten years and had become a much-appreciated counsellor to many owners. He was based in an office adjacent to the front entrance. The chintz chairs are remembered. Eric told me that LHT 716 had been the personal car of Sir William Verdon-Smith, Chairman from 1928 to 1960. He had willed the car to his doctor who, when he had stopped driving a few years later, sold the car to a Hampshire road surveyor who later advertised the car in the *Hampshire Chronicle* for £370. It was a chance purchase. We may not have been the sort of owner that G. W. had in mind. I have remembered Eric's remark: 'One day all these cars will be treasured like Bugattis are today.' I believed him then but there was no spare garage and we needed a larger car. The car went to Dave Martin, who fitted an uprated engine. LHT remains with its current Swiss owner who is now working in England with the car re-registered in England after a sojourn on Swiss plates. It was described in the November 2022 edition of *The Automobile*. The author, Toby Bruce, ferreted out my forgotten 1961 scribble in the owner's Club Bulletin about a night drive near Interlaken: 'It was as if the road was of metal and magnets were suspended from the axles. One turned the steering wheel until it seems as if all the forces were in balance and then a little more pressure on the accelerator, a little less on the wheel brought one round each successive corner.'

Above: 400 construction at Filton.

Below: 400 with Mount Blanc in the background, 1962.

400, Valencia, Spain, 1964.

Spain before the Autopistas.
Little traffic, rough surfaces.

That was a long time ago, so thank you Toby. Not forgotten was one of the first journeys in the car overnight for a weekend in Snowdonia where I was assisting with the Edinburgh Award Scheme. I felt the engine response with that direct rod linkage from pedal to carburettor and the precise movement of the oiled steering. Centaur-like, the driver becomes part of the car, experiencing the twists and turns and aware of the contours of the passing land. But then, as dawn came, I was in the mountains and down the first pass came the fears that the car would not stop. I was not alone. I later learnt Count Lurani called the early 400 the good car with the impossible brakes. After consultation with Eric Storey, Filton fitted a servo for our car. This allowed harder linings, a further improvement on earlier development work. In the 1949 Alpine Rally, after a gruelling run, Monte near victor Zdenek Treybal had not been able to stop his 400. He jumped out but his co-driver failed to get the passenger door open and the car plunged 200 feet down a ravine. Such was the strength of G. W.'s preferred bodywork that Ronnie Parkinson survived. In his lecture Jack Channer described how Filton had tackled this problem with moulded brake linings in place of woven ones. The Wellworthy Company had also created drums which stayed cooler. This work was an example of how the 400 was developed into a car whose handling, responsive controls, comfort and build quality appealed to owners who could cope with two doors and modest rear seat and legroom. In 2022 the Owner's Club listed seventy-five surviving cars.

Above: 400 drophead and Concorde.

Right: Stefan Cembrowicz's 400. This car has a 2.2-litre engine and later close ratio gearbox with overdrive. Also 406 front suspension and disc brakes.

400 tails in Australia.

3

Filton and Milan Combine:
401, 402, 403

In interviews with employees over recent years, people have frequently relayed their memories of G. W. in the factory most days talking and listening to those who were building the 400s. There was contact with owners both through correspondence and again listening when they came with their cars to Eric's Service Department. And there was pride in the competition achievements. At this distance, and from references in later letters and memos, there are indications that G. W. may have preferred to stick with the 400 whilst concentrating on developing the all-new four-door World Car. If this had been introduced as originally planned in June 1949, it would have been in advance of all other European and even world offerings.

Instead, there is Dudley Hobbs' report on the Milan visit. Even a few paragraphs impress today: 'Extremely pleasing appearance. Shape of radiator grille graceful with headlamps

The Lancia which appealed to R. V-S.

beautifully fared in. Doors front hinged. Safer and scuttle gives hinge mounting [Dudley would have had the 400 rear hinges in mind]. Construction of tubes welded together. Light alloy skin with edges beaten round the tubes. Complete with seals a suitable body would weigh about 540 lbs.' Dudley's final paragraph reads: 'The system lends itself admirably to our methods. We are familiar with tubular structures. Aluminium panels could be made more cheaply than they produce by hand in Milan. We could start as they do and gradually turn over to quantity production.' G. W. commented that the Italian body, though with larger rear seats, still only had two doors.

Although we have no record, was he thinking why interrupt and delay the development of the four-door 'World Car'? As already recorded, past difficulties had led to the Verdon-Smiths having the larger shareholding. R. V-S. liked this new concept and was supported by his father, Sir William. We cannot know what cousin car enthusiast Herbert Thomas' thinking would have been. Earlier than expected human mortality and disagreement over human behaviour both played their part in denying the planet G. W.'s ambition. Had Henry White-Smith (remembered as a Lancia enthusiast) and Herbert Thomas still been directors on the main Bristol Board this could have been a different story. In fact, there were some component supply difficulties for the successors based on the prototype car from Italy. Production of the 400 did continue until 1950 and the car carried on attracting buyers. Could it have continued till the World Car was ready?

Instead the story of Bristol Cars took a different turn. Bianchi Anderloni and his son, Carlo, had been welcomed to Filton in the summer of 1947. They had brought with them a

All-metal tube construction of 401.

complete car, which had originally been heading to AFN at Isleworth, and another partially assembled body. We do not know G. W.'s thinking but the Board's view seemed to be that here was a much more advanced body which could still make use of the 400 chassis and mechanical components. The completely new four-door car would be delayed but would still follow on. Many at Filton, including Sir Stanley, had their say. Early on it was agreed that moving the headlamps inboard adjacent to the radiator grille would give a more British look like other 1940s designs. They did not want that impression of width. A wooden buck was built to represent the Superleggera shape. Filton metalworkers fabricated an aluminium shell for what would become the 401. Whilst engine and chassis followed on from the 400, and the two-door configuration remained, all those involved wanted to update the car drawing on other available knowledge. Petrol tank and spare wheel were moved to below the floor of the luggage compartment. There was then sufficient room for R. V-S.'s golf clubs and those bigger rear seats. This tank was later found to be too far back for the best handling, as proved by Bill Banks (well known for distribution of KONI shock absorbers) when he moved the tank forward to just behind the rear seat in his successful 401 rally car.

Starting at the front of the car, they contacted Alex Moulton, remembered now for his later work with the Mini. He had been at Filton as an assistant to Roy Fedden during the war years and was then becoming known for his rubber expertise with Spencer Moulton. Alex designed shock-absorbing blocks for the front bumper, significantly visiting Filton

Sample car sent to Filton from Milan.

Above: Early 401 with ridge below doors.

Right: 401 interior – early style instruments and dashboard.

driving his Lancia Aurelia. Their continuing contact, including the chance to study the Aurelia suspension, would become important. Filton designed their own heating and ventilating system, which was effective if instructions were carefully followed, but front intakes either side of the radiator grilles are not suited to twenty-first-century traffic. Careful work went into many details. The bonnet opened from either side with pull-knob releases. Another knob behind the rear armrest unlocked the boot. Inside the boot a push button released the spare wheel tray. Yet another button in the armrest released the petrol filler cover. The doors had press button locks. John Hobbs has written of his father's commitment to eradicating any flaws in the Superleggera design. It was unsatisfactory in respect of heat and noise. Carpets, underlay, leather and other upholstery materials were most carefully chosen from suppliers. A reward for all this effort came from journalist Lawrence Pomeroy's comment in his 'Account Rendered' for 1950: 'The particular merit of the 401 is a combination of virtues which may not be equalled in any car in the world. It will comfortably carry four people and their luggage. It will sustain 80–90 mph from dawn until the cows come home and then on into the night. If unhappily one were confined to drive one car for all occasions, the Bristol would be the best buy in the world.' This praise was appreciated but the renowned LP, with one daughter, seems to have put out of mind that many, if confined to one car, would want four doors.

Sixty-three 401s (with three 402s) are recorded as sent to Australia. In December 1951, Donald Maclurcan, a Sydney architect, wrote to Filton about his 401 purchased in May. He had driven the car 3,000 miles a month when working on the Snowy Mountains Hydro-Electric Scheme. 'The wheels convey a sense of closely adhering to surfaces of all kinds while the body floats with a minimum of vertical movement. The steering remains light and lively, a sense of safety and accuracy so markedly absent from the low-geared sponginess of so many modern cars. To travel for 700 miles at an average of 57 mph and 29.98 mpg is remarkable, yet I have just done this.' That same year, Jack Lawson wrote of his trip across Canada in another 401, 'the 1,712 miles from Chicago to Calgary averaging 56 mph'. Three years later that car was in Peru. Jack described a trip to La Orya, a mining centre over the Ticlio Pass: 'I knew something of the problems of carburation at altitude

Jack Lawson's left-hand drive 401 during trans-Canada trip, 1951.

but decided to put the car at it "as is". 15,895 feet is quite a height. Provided one kept the revs up, there was still plenty of oomph. We started at 5.45 a.m. and were back home twelve hours later after 240 miles at an average 34 mph and 21 mpg over roads with pot-holed corrugated surfaces and many hairpin bends.' Filton had achieved a car that was a superb long-distance machine for the less-developed parts of the world. Those who experienced the Bristol liked what they found.

401 Around Australia Trial (Mobilgas), 1956.

401 in front of Bristol Brabazon, giant airliner.

Above: R101 Memorial. 403 with James Watt on the left.

Below: Tenth anniversary of the liberation of Bordeaux. Greetings from the Lord Mayor of Bristol.

The savage purchase tax had put paid to the 400 drophead but G. W. still reckoned that short runs of specialised models, including dropheads, might make sense provided they made use of many of the same components. After discussion with Kjell Qvale from California, Filton responded with an open two-/four-seater body for the 402. Qvale is reported to have made a loss on this first car. Filton went on to make another twenty-one of these dropheads, which have been cherished by their owners. The design has a feature which is so much appreciated when touring amidst attractive countryside. The windscreen does not have a top frame, which drivers and front passengers dislike in their line of sight – mountains then appear sectional or as if there is a permanent power cable. The side pillars were made strong enough without that frame.

The 401 and 402 were both appreciated but Bristol's Car Division was not yet making a profit. Fritz Fiedler had gladly accepted H. J.'s invitation to spend time in England (whilst BMW was getting back on its feet) to help with the new Frazer Nash sports car. He spent time at Filton. This is part of Fritz's written comment: 'The Bristol car has most of the good qualities of the BMW which I had the responsibility of designing. I compliment you on the development of the engine from a sports engine to a high-grade touring unit. A serious matter is that the car is obviously costing too much to make. The methods and rate of

402 drophead. No top frame to windscreen.

402 in New Zealand looking towards Mount Cook, South Island, New Zealand.

production are incompatible with motor manufacturing as I know it and I am confident that your costs are considerably above those of your competitors. This is understandable because they have experience you are yet to acquire. My experience has included the peculiar difficulties which arise when car production is carried out in the same factory as aircraft and aero engines. The reasons why the smooth flow of production is so difficult are because the fitting experiences could not be transmitted by drawings and reports. I was exceptionally pleased and did not expect you to make such a good car in such a short time. Those responsible are to be complimented.'

The fact remains that Laurence Pomeroy's report did not include that in 1950 the Car Division was losing £683 for every car sold. The situation was still under control. Money was still coming into the parent company from pre-fabricated housing and from the Freighter/Wayfarer sales. The Sycamore helicopter would soon be in full production. Work on the mighty Brabazon airliner would soon be suspended. G. W. still had the support of relatives – he had warned of initial losses – but he would also have been aware of the challenges of aviation. The thinking about the World Car did continue. Jan

Tony Crook at Montlhery, October 1950. One-hour run at 107 mph.

Factory photograph of new 403 without sidelights.

Lowy had talked to Fritz Feidler about the later 1930s BMW engines – about putting the camshaft higher in the block, higher than the Schleicher position – for the proposed Filton-built 3-litre. Men of business wanted easier access to spacious rear seats. Could they alter the Superleggera body? Photographer Ted Ashman took pictures of a 401-shape body still with the distinctive rear wings but with the shape of the requested four doors superimposed along the side. Meanwhile development of the Turinga-style car had continued.

By 1953 enough improvements had been introduced to merit another type number. In May the 403 was announced. Fresh air intakes could be closed. Warm air could then be recirculated improving demisting. Brake pedal operation was easier with a redesigned linkage. Engine development had increased power to 100 bhp and making the bulkhead from a denser material noticeably decreased noise transmitted to the cabin. An anti-roll bar firmly attached to the underside of the chassis frame and linking forward to the outer ends of the front suspension eliminated a slight oversteering tendency. Rear axle components were strengthened. This developed car can be recognised by a new badge on a red instead of a yellow background and '403' along the edge of the bonnet and the boot lid. Towards the end of production there were small parking lights mounted on the front wings.

The 403 is rightly cherished by owners. However, the car was still not producing a profit. Skilled workers, increasingly needed for the aircraft side, were essential for its construction and the body had only those two doors.

Later 403 with sidelights. Pre-war cars Ford, Lanchester and Standard behind.

Four doors superimposed on the shape of the 401 body.

4

British and American: 404, Arnolt, 405, 450

Whilst Jan Lowy and Fritz Fiedler were discussing the layout of the new engine, the more urgent need was to achieve a cheaper way of making current Bristol cars or their derivatives. Jack Channer had realised that around 18 inches could be taken from the chassis frame. A prototype was constructed with a central fin and two small fins on the wings. This became known as 'The Bomb'. A year or two later G. W. seems to have realised that a shorter, cheaper to make car with the appeal of two-seater status might be sold at a higher price. They were now ready to move on from the German and Italian legacies, the latter with the expensive metal tubing. They would create their own bodies. Dudley Hobbs and Jim Lane went to work with G. W. and were very hands on, consulting at every stage. Instead of the tubing the lower structure was built up with steel framework and aluminium panels. A now wooden canopy for the roof and window

Building a wooden canopy which was placed on top of the metal lower structure of the 404.

area fitted on top. Woodworking skills were less in demand by other divisions of the company. The previous body design had the heavy spare wheel low down at the back. Why not put this in the same place as many pre-war cars alongside the engine? With a long bonnet enclosing machinery well back for the best weight distribution, there was just room for the spare between the wheel arch and door leading edge. It was reached by lifting the upward-opening cover. In a similar compartment the other side went battery and electrical components. There was no longer allegiance to the BMW grille, so they evolved their own air intake. Nor did they persevere with their costly heating and ventilating system. A standard Smith's system was purchased. It was fitted in front of the screen between two barriers which help to keep engine heat away from the passenger compartment. This double barrier became a much-appreciated feature of all the following six-cylinder cars.

The smaller short-chassis car, the 404, with some of the outline of the Bomb, is today the most valuable (except for the one-offs or special bodies) of the six-cylinder Bristols. At the time there were rave reports. Michael Brown wrote in *The Autocar*: 'Very occasionally the wine of experience overflows the glass of expectation and the would-be connoisseur is aware that he has approached perfection. Nearly two thousand miles with a 404 has left me the memory of one of those rare satisfactions.' Of the short stick gear lever, which had replaced the earlier less-precise wand and had been fitted to later 403s, Michael

Side view of the 404 on runway at Filton. Short wheelbase is evident.

wrote: 'The action might be jewelled after a dozen changes just using the tips of three fingers. Another transmission feature is the free wheel which permits changes into the lowest gear with greater facility than synchromesh.' Not every owner was so enthusiastic. Drivers were finding that these short wheelbase cars could be affected by changes in wind pressure, for instance a gap in a hedgerow or when passing a coach or high-sided lorry. The aerofoil shape of the body lifted the rear of the car. A Swedish owner persuaded Ford to put a 404 in their Cologne wind tunnel. At 100 mph the rear wheels were barely in contact with the surface beneath.

The Bomb was kept for experimental work including the development of the Watt link suspension. Another Watt, James, no relation, who had undertaken sales and testing journeys for Donald Healey and then Austin, had been appointed Sales Manager in 1952. A sales tour of Canada and the USA had not been fruitful. As Sir William Welsh, SMMT representative based in Washington, explained in a letter to G. W.: 'The Americans are reluctant to pay a much higher price for offerings with less room than their own products. Also in the West distances between towns are very great and the road surfaces perfect. They would not appreciate the Bristol handling and control. In the East there are rigidly enforced speed limits.' A left-hand drive saloon did win a magnificent trophy for the best four-seater, 2-litre saloon at the New York Show in 1953. Over the following two years six 403s, two 404s and eleven 405s were sold in America.

Tony Crook racing 404 at BARC members' meeting, Goodwood, 1954.

James Watt looking toward camera. 403 without sidelights. On the left is Andre Charbonnet, distributor in France.

403 and 404 together. Typical Filton-style publicity shot.

However, there is another story to be told. At the show James Watt met up with S. H. Arnolt, based in Warsaw, Indiana. 'Wacky' Arnolt's manufacturing enterprise had profited from the war. Post-war he had established a showroom in Chicago to distribute the likes of Bentley, MG and Rolls-Royce. He had already imported Bertone-bodied MGs and he explained to James that he was looking for another chassis, preferably British, which could also be fitted with a two-seat body by Bertone in Italy and then sold at an acceptable price in America. Whilst consultation had not been possible, G. W. was the sort of person who listened when James returned to Filton with this idea. He realised that the short 404 chassis could be ideal for the job and such sales could be a good source of income. It was back to another Anglo-Italian partnership.

On 27 April 1953 James Watt met up with Arnolt and Bertone in Turin. On 11 May Arnolt came to Filton and four days later the contract was signed. Bristol would send examples

Right: Arnolt rarely seen with hood.

Below: Arnolt side view at Filton.

of the 404 chassis by ferry and train to Turin. Spring rates and steering column rake were altered. 403 brakes with the earlier 11-inch brake drums and the longer gear lever were surplus anyway. Bertone created that charismatic shape which disguised the tall BS1 MK2 engine. The body was made in steel rather than aluminium partly on account of strength but also to make repair work easier for American panel beaters. Records confirm that 141 cars were sent to Turin and then shipped to America. The majority were upholstered in a plastic material, though twenty-eight cars had Filton's exquisite leatherwork recorded in beige, blue, brown, grey, maroon, red or white. Chassis No. 3083 was built as a fixed head coupe and displayed at the 1954 Paris Show. No. 3121 was another fixed head coupe displayed at Earl's Court. These two had wind-up windows and swivelling quarter lights. Records also show Arizona, California, Georgia, Illinois, Michigan, New Jersey, New York, Oklahoma and Utah where some of the cars were sold. There's an evocative note in a file found that reads: 'Deliver three cars to Rootes Motors. When you get close enough to Long Island City telephone to find out the exact address where the cars (and a Hillman Californian with white walls) are to be unloaded.' Arnolt Bristols were much enjoyed by their drivers on the racetracks of America – Elkhart Lakes, Sebring, Watkins Glen, etc. G. W.'s support for this venture gave pleasure to many American drivers and to the spectators who flocked to the circuits.

Packing Arnolt chassis to send to Turin.

In his talk to the Owner's Club in 1975 Jack Channer explained that thinking about a new chassis for the larger four-door saloon and the bigger engine had at last started in 1952. The World Car was finally underway. They still saw no need to rush the work; they wanted every detail to be right. The family were still supporting G. W. The Arnolt had produced a worthwhile return and the short-chassis 404 showed how they could now make a composite wood and metal body with less call on the aeroplane workforce. Following on the four-door mock-up seen in pictures being worked out on a 401/403-type body, they next extended the 404 shape to create a four-door body on the original chassis length. With wide rear doors there would be good access to the back seats. This became the 405. There are comments that, in pursuit of that rear access for the working Executive, the front doors were made too narrow.

This was not a problem for a driver of G. W.'s stature but not so good for the tall driver. The door bottoms were also too low so that, with a high curb, it may not be possible to get out of the car. Cost was reduced with the bought-in heating system, as in the 404, and other fittings like door handles, hinges and bumpers. An overdrive, which had previously been fitted on some earlier cars on request, was now standard, enabling motorway (or trans-Africa) cruising at lower engine revs. With the original chassis length and side-mounted spare (as in the 404), and the petrol tank above the rear axle, Filton had worked out a larger and convenient luggage space. Potential buyers now had the four doors, which benefited family

Extended wooden canopy of 405 to provide room for four doors. 404 behind.

and business use, whilst still enjoying the response and feel and quality as they drove. They also had a car of appealing shape suggestive of unfettered travel to distant destinations. From the driving seat, the central air scoop with gullies either side between the bonnet and the well-defined front wings assist accurate positioning on the road. This is so noticeable in contrast to cars in which the driver cannot see the extremity of the wing. Instruments, following the 404, now in a nacelle above the steering wheel, and in the driver's line of sight, added to the 'in command' feeling. The 405 pointed to what they hoped the four-door World Car, whose chassis was now coming so good on test, would soon offer.

Introduced at the 1954 Paris Show, there was alarm when the demonstration 405 overheated in heavy Paris traffic. Back at Filton, aiming for sufficient cooling in all markets, the central spotlight was deleted from export cars. The fan designed for the World Car was also fitted. Andre Charbonnet went on to sell thirty-four 405s in France. Eight of these were dropheads. He had also sold twenty 401s and eighteen 403s and went on to sell thirteen 406s. We visited the Chardonnet Service Station in rue Etienne-Marcel in 1964 (driving the 406 prototype TLN). There were six-cylinder 406s in the service bays including the Beutler 406. We were given a leaflet listing Bristol agents in Bordeaux, Cannes, Lille and Lyon. Other agents were in Brussels, Copenhagen, Geneva, Lisbon and Madrid. We were also shown a letter from a prominent French lawyer: 'The 405 had been driven 40,000 kms

Left-hand drive 405 without central spotlight and larger overriders for the Paris Show, 1957.

in two years often travelling 350 kms at a good pace and at one point the speedometer showing 180 kmh.'

The part-wood body frames of the 404 and the 405, which would fill the gap till the all-new car was ready, were not so well received in Australia. Donald Maclurcan, who had been so enthusiastic about the steel-framed 401, wrote about the 404: 'Timber is not suitable for bodywork here. Doors have dropped and moved backwards. There are advancing cracks in the panelling at the base of the pillars.' G. W. personally replied: 'The crack at the base of the windscreen is quite new.' His letter was backed up by Eric Storey: 'Fear for the joint

Right: 405 with J. H. Bradburn of Bradburn and Wedge.

Below: Interior of 405. Saloon chrome switch for overdrive to right of instruments.

between the scuttle and the screen framework.' Records list a 405 saloon sold by Glasby's garage in Southern Rhodesia in 1957. The owner must have been Keith Simmonds. Here is an edited version of what he wrote for the Club Bulletin published in winter 1966:

> Salisbury in Rhodesia is a bit further from the sea than its Wiltshire namesake, but by pointing the 405 eastwards and keeping going for 340 miles, we can dip into the ocean at Beira. Up early so no worries about night driving and the consequent animal hazards. Driving at speeds which the road invites can be a costly business due to speed limits. It is still feasible to tuck away 60 miles into every hour until the Portuguese border. From Umtali onwards comfort is the only guide to speed. As the road varies from excellent to diabolical, the needle ranges from a gentle caress of the 90 mph point to a lurch in sympathy with depressions up to a foot in depth that make 50 mph a better proposition. Some miles from the Coast the Pungwe River flats change the vista to miles of low-lying land. The last few miles into Beira are bumpy but the sea air is in the lungs and, of course, the carburettors. As the engine is tuned for 5,000 feet above sea level, pinking creeps in until a flick of the hand retards the spark a fraction. The return trip is much the same. A late lunch in Umtali allows a rest before the last leg takes us home arriving with darkness about 6pm. Last trip 31.2 mpg.

It seems likely that this was the car whose remains I saw in the 1970s. A 405 sent back from Central Africa for general overhaul had to be scrapped because termites had eaten the wooden frame members. They had been right to see these cars as interim products awaiting the all-metal World Car. From 1954 to 1957, 262 405 saloons were built at Filton. Bristol also contracted with coachbuilders E. D. Abbott at Farnham to build forty-two drophead 405s. Filton sent the chassis with bonnet and front wings. Talking with ex-Abbott craftsmen in 2008 they explained that two saloon rear wings came with the cars. A new section had to be added to the front of the wings to match up with the changed door post location. They told me that the aluminium used by Bristol was a hard 16-gauge aircraft-type alloy which was difficult to weld without cracking. They had had to ask Filton to send appropriate welding rods. They also mentioned that, after Abbott had received the contract from Ford to make estate car conversions of the Consul, Zephyr, Zodiac range, they thought some of these Bristol bodies were made by Tickford, another coachbuilder with whom Abbott were associated. Together with the short-chassis 404s, these dropheads have become the most highly valued Bristol-engined cars. Geoffrey Herdman who, with his wife, Hilary, has magnificently driven their drophead right round the world, has commented on the value of the front window quarter light. Unlike some other cars, this swings right round to stream fresh air towards the driver's face, a feature much appreciated when they were in Central America. And, a minor but interesting detail, the drophead quarter light is larger than on the saloon. A special order came from Saudi Arabia for a car with a hydraulically operated hood. This would not have been difficult for Abbott as they had made nineteen Mk 6 Bentleys with powered hoods. It was definitely Abbott which made the one 404 drophead. This had a front-hinged bonnet. The spare wheel was in the consequent open side well rather than reached via an upward-opening cover.

Above: White drophead 405.

Below: 10 DPG in South America.

10 DPG at the RAC. Honoured after the world trip.

What follows is not primarily concerned with the passenger cars, the subject of this book, but it is an important part of the balance sheet. British sports and racing car makers, as well as Arnolt in America, had observed that the 2-litre Bristol engine was not only producing lots of power but that it was also comparatively light in weight. The requests to purchase these engines was accepted by G. W. This would follow on from the contract with AFN to supply the FNS specification engines for the Frazer Nash and details are recorded in a later chapter. The author has not forgotten watching Mike Hawthorn's meteoric 1952 Goodwood start in the black Cooper Bristol nor observing Eric Storey, pipe in mouth, bending over the engine as he checked the carburettors! There is a picture of G. W. at Silverstone in discussion with John Cooper and a Cooper Bristol. In the background are 401 saloons with racing numbers. All the six-cylinder cars up to and including the four-door 405 saloons competed in production car races. Tony Crook, who was later to play such a large part in developing and preserving the Bristol marque, was one of the leading spirits in this enterprise on the circuits.

Back in 1948 Leslie Johnson had purchased what remained of Raymond Mays' pre-war ERA concern. After other commissions, his designers, led by David Hodkin, produced a potential Grand Prix contender, the G type. Whilst working on their own power unit, they asked Bristol for one of their racing engines for Formula 2. Then Leslie Johnson became ill

Mike Hawthorn in Cooper Bristol at Goodwood.

George White
and John Cooper
at Goodwood.

Stanley White at Goodwood with John Cooper behind.

and in October 1952 it was announced that the Bristol Aeroplane Company's Car Division had purchased ERA and their G type. A racing department had already been set up with Vivian Selby in charge. G. W., still fully supported by R. V-S., decided to enter a Bristol team for the 1953 24 Hours of Le Mans race. The hoped for success, even just participation, would bring the Bristol name to a wider public before the advent of the World Car. The G type became the basis for Dave Summer's chassis development. The chassis tubes were made

ERA from which 450 was developed.

Above: One of the first 450s on the runway at Filton.

Below: 450 from the front, 1954. Fairings for all lights.

from steel in place of magnesium alloy. Bristol created new coupe bodywork, not an object of beauty but this first version had to be put together quickly in time to satisfy the race regulations. The by then legendary Percy Kemish, with thirty years' experience going back to the Bentleys at Le Mans in the 1920s and then Lagonda's courageous foray in 1939, came to Filton. He was soon joined by Stan Ivermee with similar background experience. They concentrated on engine development for continuous high-speed use.

There was some conflict. Bristol Engines had reckoned that the crankshafts needed balance weights to reduce out of balance forces on the main bearings at continuous high revs for twenty-four hours. Some years later Percy Kemish explained: 'Neither Stan nor I were happy with these weights and said so, but, after so long on the test bed without trouble, we had no evidence to justify our complaints.' They were able to consult with Stuart Tresilian, another legendary figure, who had worked on car and aero engines at Rolls-Royce in the 1930s and then moved to Lagonda in the years just before the war. He was now a consultant on other projects with the Bristol parent company. He too expressed his concern about these weights, but was not in a position to order their removal. Two 450s, with Percy and Stan in the supporting team, started in the 1953 Le Mans race. Neither car finished. On the test bed engines had been accelerated smoothly. In racing conditions reversals of load during gear changes caused torsional crankshaft vibration. The fixings of the balance weights broke so that they became missiles of destruction. Percy, Stan and Stuart's concerns had been correct.

Building the team in the workshops at Filton.

With hindsight there is reflection on the consequence of car components having been made by separate divisions. On the other hand, the wealth of engineering experience and knowledge at Filton has led to later engines being outstanding examples of internal combustion design. And earlier engines can now be brought up to the same standard of excellence.

G. W. was not deterred by this experience. A month later the repaired cars were at Rheims without those weights. One of them won the 2-litre class of the Twelve Hour Race. Three revised cars were entered for Le Mans in 1954 and, in bad weather, finished seventh, eighth and ninth winning the 2-litre class. At Rheims they won the team prize. Racing engine builder Ray Williams, talking years later, remembered the enormous care with which a Le Mans engine was built up: 'All the parts were in a rack. You were on your own, responsible from start to finish till the job was done.' For the 1955 Le Mans the cars were converted to open bodies and again finished seventh, eighth and ninth. This was the year of the ghastly Levegh crash. G. W. donated Bristol's prize money to the disaster fund. The racing team had served its purpose. Sir Robert Wall wrote: 'Everyone at Filton took a proprietorial interest in the enterprise and its fortunes. The vans which were the mobile support shops always attracted a crowd before their departure for an international event.' But then that autumn 1955 there were other concerns. There was steady progress on the World Car but the whole arena of the Bristol Aeroplane Company was going to have to be reorganised.

Mechanics at Le Mans, 1954. Vivian Selby behind 33 and Percy Kemish by the door of 34.

Above: 450 racing at Rheims, 1954. Mike Keane and Trevor Line on way to tenth place.

Below: Le Mans 1955, driven by Peter Wilson and Jim Mayers. Note Citroens, Renaults and Simcas in the car park.

Above: 1954. Percy Kemish talking to G.W., Dave Summers in the middle and on the right Rupert Gildersleeve, Ken Evans, Dave Wilkins and Charlie Bush.

Below: Group at Filton. Back row, third from left: Stan Sparkes, Rupert Gildersleeve, Charlie Bush, Albert Bromley, Ken Evans, Dave Wilkins, Maskell, Gray Ross. Front row: Dave Summers, Stan Ivermee, Mabel Selby, Percy Kemish and Vivian Selby.

George White and Vivian Selby back at Filton after the 1955 Le Mans.

5

New Designs to Challenge BMW and Mercedes: Projects 220/240 and 225

There have already been references to Jack Channer's lecture to the Owner's Club when he talked about the early development of the new chassis frame, particularly the front suspension. What Jack went on to say, together with my own conversations with Alex Moulton, are sources of information about the construction and rigorous testing of the World Car prototype, the 220, later renamed as the 240. Jack described so many details.

220 chassis made with 14-gauge steel.

He started by explaining that 14-gauge steel was used for the chassis. This was stiffer than the BMW derivatives. The centre cross-member was 6 x 4.5 inches rectangular in place of 3-inch tube. All joints were internally webbed, a significant contribution to stiffness. The front cross-member, only bolted in the BMW descendents, was welded. Remembering the 401/403 handling tendencies that had been improved by the fuel tank relocation in the 405, there was much thought given to tank positioning. The aim is always maximum traction and minimum intrusion into luggage space. Starting with four rear chassis cross-members, the space between them provided a cavity for the petrol tank located immediately in front of the rear axle. The top and the front of the cavity were covered by the seat pan and the heel board behind the feet of rear passengers. What Jack called a skirt piece, on which the final drive support casting was mounted, formed the back of this cavity. A detachable bracing below the tank made up the fourth side of the cavity and provided protection on rough road surfaces. As with the former BMW-based car, there was again no heavy chassis frame to the rear of the axle. Instead, the light monocoque boot construction made full use of strong wheel arches. Careful design had allowed 30 gallons of petrol to be carried in an auxiliary tank in that boot. This had enabled long mileages for testing purposes in the prototype car without having to stop to take on more petrol.

220 chassis. Petrol tank in front of rear axle, inboard disc brakes.

Jack then explained in his lecture that Filton had kept in touch with Alex Moulton who had worked as assistant to Roy Fedden during the war. It was Alex who had designed the rubber shock absorber mount for the 401 front bumper. Alex's great-grandfather, Stephen Moulton, had met up with Charles Goodyear in America. He had brought the rubber vulcanisation process to England in the nineteenth century. In partnership with George Spencer, they had pioneered the use of rubber springs for railway carriages. Now Alex's aim was to produce new rubber suspension for cars dependent on the chemical bonding of rubber to metal. This bonding allows the rubber to be used in shear. Alex himself explained: 'I was interested in the rubber torsion bush, an inner shaft and outer metal sleeve, with rubber in the annular space, being bonded to the two metal surfaces. Twisting the shaft deflects the rubber. If the load to be sprung is carried on an arm attached to the shaft, there is a suspension device.'

Alex called this device 'Flexitor'. In 1952 they were fitted to the little Bond Minicar remembered as having a better-than-expected ride, mainly due to the 'Flexitors'. They were then an important contribution to the Austin Gypsy project. Two years later, in 1954, with G. W.'s agreement, Jack decided on using 'Flexitors' for the 220 rear suspension with skewed trailing arms similar to the Lancia Aurelia. Alex Moulton had been visiting Filton

220 showing housing for Flexitor rubber front suspension.

in his Aurelia, so there is likely to have been further consultation about that design. Jack commented that the car went well from the start with a very flat ride and little roll. Worries about hot and cold climates were soon dispelled. The front suspension started with coil springs, was changed to torsion bars and then ended up with Flexitor on the front as well. Jack further explained: 'As a passenger I remember looking out of the rear window of the car when it was driven hard on a winding road. I could not detect any significant roll when aligning that window visually against the road behind.' Meeting up some years later on a visit to Bradford-on-Avon, Alex Moulton told the author that he had been thrilled by the car's ride. There are notes and diagrams in the Moulton archives which confirm that this prototype completed 75,000 miles of satisfactory running. Jack said that the Moulton

220 Flexitor, steering rack and front anti-roll bar.

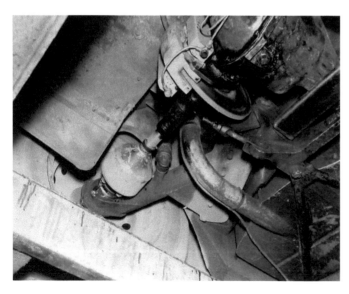

220 petrol tank, rear axle, Flexitor unit and inboard disc brake.

suspension never gave any trouble at all. Speaking twenty years later, he reckoned the 220 rode like the then modern, i.e., 1970s, Mercedes 220 or 2-litre BMW. 'It was very safe,' he concluded. Jack also mentioned details such as a steering column adjustable for rake and seats adjustable for height as well as reach.

Mike Newall took over the 220/240 project when Jack Channer left Filton in 1955. The prototype had first been run with a Bristol engine and then with several second-hand Jaguar units. Of interest, Bristol insisted on testing these Jaguar engines and found them well down on the advertised power output. Meanwhile Jan Lowy, keeping in mind his discussions with Fritz Feidler, had been working on the design of the 3-litre overhead camshaft engine before he moved to Ford. Then there was the legendary Stuart Tresilian already mentioned and working on other Filton projects. His vast engine design experience included the 3 1/2-litre Bentley, the Phantom Three and the V Twelve Lagonda. Stuart was on hand for consultation with Jan and also with Gary O'Neill when he joined the Bristol team from Rolls-Royce and took over the development of the new engine. Denis Sevier worked on many of the details as part of the team. Percy Kemish, working with Stan Ivermee, had worked so hard to perfect the original 2-litre. They were also on hand a little longer before retirement. Between them, and under G. W.'s guidance, they decided to increase capacity to 3.65 litres. It was a courageous decision to create a lighter all-aluminium power unit.

3.65-litre engine in final form.

This could then be mounted forward over the suspension without affecting steering and handling. The front seats were then also further forward in the chassis than in the 2-litre cars. Moving to the rear, it then followed that the shaped rear seats could also be forward with a comfortable angle for the backrest and sufficient legroom; this was also helped by the position of the petrol tank. Such was the genesis of the four-door car in which all four occupants would have been able to relax on long journeys. There had been no attempt to create a five-seater.

Here at last was the potentially world-beating four-door car. Within the whole Bristol organisation there were the skills to achieve the bodywork. Records confirm that in the early 1950s Bristol Aeroplane bought more land and were planning to build a complete new factory for car production. All seemed set fair: the delay resulting from the two-door 401/403 creations did not matter. Those in their own way superb products had not brought profit but they had burnished the Bristol Car name as a consequence of the worldwide sales. Then came enormous problems on the aeroplane side. Disastrously for this whole tale, the planned new car factory was not started. Again the previous Fiedler comment 'peculiar difficulties when car production is in the same factory as aircraft and aero engines' comes forcefully to mind. In 1954 two de Havilland Comet airliners had disintegrated in mid-flight (subsequently found in one plane to be caused by a crack growing from a rivet hole but they had all suffered from sudden loss of pressurization). Tests showed that the window shape was to blame.

World Car/220 chassis on Filton runway. 404 beyond. With forward mounting enabled by the aluminium engine, rear seats could be forward of the axle.

Government reaction was that all new aircraft had to undergo stress tests equivalent to a plane's whole life cycle. This applied to the Aeroplane Company's superb new Britannia airliner, although there was no evidence of any similar potential problems. This meant there would be delays in delivery. Payment for the planes from the airline purchasers would also be delayed. The whole Bristol organisation's income would be considerably reduced. Hindsight is temptingly easy. If the Whites, Stanley and George, had had as large a shareholding as the Verdon-Smiths and if they had decided against the Superleggera route, would the Moulton suspension prototype have been ready for production a vital year, or even two years, earlier? It is a striking example of the difficulties which beset brave industrial entrepreneurs. In the delay resulting from the determination to perfect the car, which could have then been ahead of the field for the next twenty years or more, G. W. found himself up against insuperable difficulties caused by mistakes made in other industries.

R. V-S.'s response to these events was recorded in the autumn 1955 issue of the Bristol Aeroplane Company Review. From January 1956, instead of Divisions, there were to be three separate Companies: Bristol Aircraft, Bristol Aero Engines and Bristol Cars. G. W. would be Chairman and Managing Director of Bristol Cars Ltd. One of the head office accountants would also be a Director. R. V-S. would no longer be involved with the cars. There was now no possibility of building the World Car in quantity in a new Bristol factory. This was the reality which had to be faced but the car was so advanced in concept, as Jack Channer said, like a 1970s product, that it seems G. W. and colleagues felt it was worth continuing the engine development in the hope that there could still somehow be production in the future. Denis Sevier was working with Smith's Industries on a new gearbox using magnetised metal particles which could operate manually or as an automatic. At Filton Denis had also designed a five-speed manual box. With the use of aluminium the new type 160 engine was much lighter than the Jaguar. On the test bed in 1956 examples of these engines were taken up to and continuously run at 6,200 rpm. This was testing way beyond the stresses of everyday use. There is a note in the records that one of the engineers then involved has kindly lent: 'One engine had "burst" its crankcase.' This was not seen as a disaster. It was ensuring that faults were eliminated before the new cars were in the hands of customers. Far from then giving up the project, as has been suggested in other accounts, a further note records: 'The test house must be enlarged so that three 160 engines can be run at full power.' Gray Ross was recruited to assist Gary O'Neil. Together they did successfully carry on the testing, eventually running engines at full power for long periods.

It was Gray Ross who compiled a report dated May 1957 for circulation to G. W., D. E. Hobbs, S. S. Tresilian, D. W. Sevier and P. H. Frith (assistant chief metallurgist of Bristol Aero Engines). Gray explained how shell bearings rely on their housing for support. The problem had been keeping the aluminium bearing housings within the design limits of the drawings. In this innovative use of this lighter material, the aluminium was distorting as it expanded. It was realised that it was important to give much more time to the preparation of the metal including stress relief. The Vandervell company had been helpful and it was decided that they would do more work on these new Bristol engines in their own factory. Some months later Gray Ross reported that it had been agreed 'that bearing bores would be machined and the shells fitted by Messrs Vandervell'.

Outside the Sofitel, Queenstown, New Zealand: 403, 402, 2 x 400, 405.

Engine faults were not the reason for the demise of the potential World Car. Other continuing improvements were recorded that summer. Examples are a new sintered bronze bush for the chain tension adjustment, fan pulleys in steel rather than aluminium, and a new water outlet now at the back of the cylinder head. As the pictures show, the new engine was coming good, more powerful but also lighter, enabling the more forward mounting. Details visible are familiar to existing 2-litre owners, the precise accelerator linkage, neat valve cover fixings, accessible filter and distributor. An engine can be seen mounted in the chassis but whether it was connected up to enable movement is not known. It was other problems and the financial consequences for Bristol Aeroplane which stopped the work on the Moulton chassis and this engine, both with great potential.

Nor were Bristol Cars able to proceed with another project which could have been a good companion to the 3.6-litre saloon. Writing from Canada, Ken Oakes has told me about a proposed two-seater using an engine embracing all the Le Mans experience which G. W. had asked him to consider. Ken sent copies of drawings dated 1954. Working with Jack Channer until Jack left Filton, this was to be an open car based on the 404. They opted for double wishbone front suspension instead of the BMW transverse leaf with Salter laminated torsion bars providing the front springs. This meant that the front cross-member could be in much lighter aluminium. The rear suspension was to use the Watt link which had been developed on 'The Bomb' and was soon to be used again in the 406. There would be rear torsion bars and long shock absorbers with a high upper mounting. James Watt tried to interest Wacky Arnolt in this Project 225 as a follow on from the earlier Arnolt. He was not successful. Bristol Cars now concentrated on further BMW layout development to produce another saloon car when they realised that they could not complete the 'Moulton' prototype. G. W. had many loyal customers and was determined to continue.

6

George White's Bristol Cars Ltd: The 2.2-litre 406

The three new companies began as separate entities in January 1956. They were still subsidiaries of the Bristol Aeroplane Company, which retained overall control. With the Britannia airliner Bristol had an aeroplane acknowledged to be superb. Robert Wall's book 'Bristol Aircraft' confirms that interest from the Airlines was intense. He explains 'A Britannia then experienced "flame-out" on all four engines in extremely rare cloud conditions over Uganda. The reason was the build-up of ice in the bends of the Proteus engine intakes. Stanley Hooker quickly devised glow plugs to immediately re-light the engines in such conditions.' (The bends were originally incorporated as protection against water spray in the Princess flying boats, an example of how decisions can have unexpected consequences.)

There had already been the delays resulting from the Comet testing. Now, for two years, BOAC refused to accept and pay for the Britannias till yet more tests had been completed. Other customers hesitated. Stocks of this attractive smooth flying machine (the author flew back from Rhodesia in one in 1956) built up at Filton. If searching for a predominant reason why Bristol cars are not in the spaces occupied by Mercedes and BMW, it is here. The magnificent completed Britannias remained at Filton with no income from sales. The market was open to Boeing and their 707. It was nearly the end of the whole company and it was the end of any possibility of assistance to or investment in Bristol Cars. The next event was government insistence on amalgamation of Bristol Aero engines with Hawker Siddeley to form Bristol Siddeley in 1958. This was demanded before they would receive an engine contract. In this new cocktail those who had amassed the larger shareholding as a consequence of family history wanted Bristol Cars to become a subsidiary of Bristol Siddeley instead of Bristol Aeroplane.

There were then some press references to the possibility of making new Bristol Siddeley cars. A Sapphire 346 engine was installed in an early example of the next car, the 406. The result was too much weight over the transverse leaf front suspension. Also the bulkhead behind the Bristol engines had to be cut away resulting in much more cabin heat. This just was not a starter. Instead the reality is shown by some notes handwritten by another Director, probably Brian Davidson, before the first Board meeting, which the author was fortunate to find when searching through old file cabinets. These cabinets had been cast aside in a disused part of a Patchway factory next to Filton. Some kind informants knew of their existence. The notes firmly state: 'Should pull out of Bristol Cars closing down the activity unless it should be disposed of by the end of March.' At the Board meeting on 19 January 1960 it was proposed 'that Bristol Cars should be shut off as quickly, conveniently and cheaply as possible'. R. V-S. was in the chair. G. W., not a Director, was not present. This was a different relationship to the days of joint negotiation with H. J. Aldington involving R. V-S. fifteen years earlier.

When all this was reported to G. W. he did not want to stop production. He did not want those who had joined him at the start to have to look for new jobs; nor did he want to let down those owners who liked the cars or lose the servicing relationships with close customer contact. G. W. dug into his own resources and savings. He was joined by Anthony Crook, a Bristol dealer based in the London area who had been increasingly helpful in the sale of cars. Together they took on the ownership of Bristol Cars, G. W. holding 60 per cent and Anthony Crook 40 per cent. The accountants explained to the Bristol Siddeley Board that 'whilst taxation would be worse if they were not closed down, they would be relieved of any risk from potentially dead stock and would not have to use space for storage or the operation of the spares service'. This was accepted. Bristol Cars became G. W.'s own company. After negotiation they moved out of the former Shield Laundry building and back to the Light Engineering Division premises.

G. W. had also accepted that they could not continue with the four-door World Car prototype even though hindsight suggests that the car would have been well received in many countries who had come to appreciate the virtues of the earlier cars, and there were many well-established UK dealers in full support who had achieved many sales (see Appendix). The whole concept was still far ahead of its time and it seems likely that the Bristol Board would have got their money back and gone on to receive handsome profits. Sadly, almost tragically, such are the affairs of humankind, it was not to be. Instead one Mervyn Broomfield, who then worked at Filton, offered to purchase the 240 without powertrain or any Bristol identification for a small sum. He would look after the innovative

Partially clothed chassis some years later at Littlestoke.

chassis plus Moulton suspension with the hope that some future for this inspired concept might still evolve. It was taken to Mervyn's garage at Littlestoke. He had begun to build up a body when he sadly died in a fall at the nuclear power station for which he was then working. The 240 was returned to Filton. In time the storage space was needed. What was left of the project had to be scrapped.

With a smaller workforce and much less factory space they had to think again. If the World Car was not possible and production numbers were to be much lower than they had previously envisaged, G. W. realised that the two-door concept could be acceptable. This thinking led to the 406. There were older affluent drivers, whose family had grown

Scale models. Alternative rear window designs for World Car.

TLN, the prototype 406, in first light grey colour scheme.

up and moved on. Rear seat entry was less important. Easy access to the two front seats would be welcomed. The consequent large doors also meant large windows with vision uninterrupted by side pillars. Such customers would appreciate interiors with comfort and convenience, which would justify a higher price. It was back to some of the original thinking, a smaller car to Bentley standard for those who did not want or need the size of the larger Bentley product. The two-door Bentleys with bodies built by Mulliner and Park Ward cost almost twice as much. In April 1960, with purchase tax, the 406 was £4,244, the Mulliner Bentley was £8,119 and James Young £8,197. The 401 and 403, if not as it seems G. W.'s preferred choice, had shown there was a limited market for a high-quality two-door car. That sort of production number, 275 for the 403, was more in line with what the new company might be able to achieve.

All the knowledge they had all gained over the past ten years went into the development of the 406 chassis. Starting at the back there was the rear axle link which Jack Channer had initiated for the Bomb and which Ken Oakes had then considered for the 225 two-seater.

Above: TLN front interior showing seat-reclining mechanism.

Left: TLN rear interior storage pockets either side of seat.

This Watt link had already been tested on a 405. Its initiator, James Watt, is on record as writing to Matthew Boulton in 1784: 'I have a glimpse of a method of causing a piston rod to move up and down perpendicularly.' In the Bristol application an upright lever is pivoted on the rear of the 406's differential casing. Both ends of this rocking lever are attached to arms which are also pivoted on mountings on the car's structure. A further radius arm runs forward from the top of the casing to restrain twisting under torque. Thus true vertical movement is achieved. This gives the feeling of stability which is such an endearing feature of these cars. Even in appalling conditions caused by weather or road surface the 406 maintains its course. The rear axle was changed to a bought-out Salisbury hypoid unit and hub bearings now needed to be greased by gun. The new braking system was developed by Dunlop and would have been used on the World Car. This was one of the first applications of disc brakes on all four wheels. Braking was assisted by a servo unit easily accessible via the off-side lift-up wing flap.

They were also working to still make fullest use of the ex-BMW engine. There was enough room to increase the size of the bores in the cylinder block so that, with larger pistons and a longer stroke, the total capacity would be 2.2 litres. Some of Gray Ross' written reports dated October 1957 have been found: 'The oldest 2.2-litre. Very extensive full throttle running on the test bed. Used to investigate alternative SU carburettors. Eventually seizure of Number 1 piston. It was concluded that some of the running clearances could have been taken up by cylinder surface irregularities.' Also: 'Discussion with Wellworthy, manufacturers of piston rings, led to suggestion of slotted oil control rings which would have less severe oil control properties. Wellworthy were prepared to supply, for development use, a set of pistons with an altered profile.' Another conclusion was that, whilst the SU carburettors were easier to tune, the SOLEX, when correctly tuned,

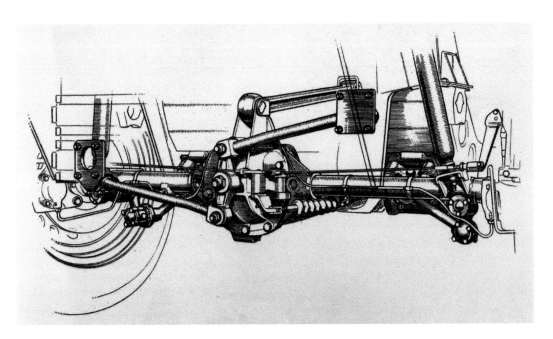

Rear axle with Watt linkage.

406 2.2-litre engine.

gave a better response. Obviously life would be easier with a larger-capacity engine but that, as Ken Oakes had worked out, would mean considerable alteration to the front of the car. Without the World Car, those at Filton were working to maximise the value of the BMW legacy. Bristol Engines agreed to continue making this engine for a few more years.

Jack Channer had sought other challenges. Dudley Hobbs continued to lead the team which created that new two-door body. Having owned and driven a 406 for fifty years, and the prototype before that, the author finds it difficult to contain his praise. Having ditched the 405's curb-hitting four doors, those two resulting large replacements stop at sill level. There is a fixed panel beneath so curbs are no longer hit or can prevent opening. Ventilation remains a lesson to other manufacturers. With the large air intake in front of the screen fully open, large single side windows wound right down and the two rear extractor windows opened securely on their catches, travel can be at motorway or autoroute cruising speeds without any of the buffeting which affects so many designs in this century. Few other manufacturers seem to have tried to achieve this exquisite window open experience crossing Continents or traversing the Highlands, breathing in fresh air and the different passing smells and scents. Manipulation of the four rotating knobs can bring sufficient warm air to prevent interior screen mist in winter and sufficient cool air in summer. It is an exceptionally efficient system without the need for the complications of air conditioning – which also has to be recharged.

G. W. and his colleagues had sensibly realised that a partial wood framework as in the 405 was not the best answer; also they were not going to have the factory space to

Above: After 80,000 miles with R. V-S., purchased by author early 1960s. Here in Majorca with view of unique tail and rear fins.

Below: South of France, now painted darker grey with silver roof. Contrast Peugeots of that era.

make complete bodies in acceptable numbers? The full story is not known. It seems they searched around and found the Jones Brothers at the Albion Works near Old Oak Common railway sidings in Willesden. Jones had been making ambulances and pick-ups, the name given to car-like vehicles with open truck-like compartments behind the rear seats. There had been praise for the finish on the open-top Humber Super Snipes they had created for the 1953 Royal Commonwealth Tour. If Bristol could get the 406 chassis to London, Jones would complete the inner body structure and the aluminium panelling to the Hobbs design. The cars would then be sent back to Filton where there would still be space for the Bristol craftsmen to continue with their upholstery work and other furnishing. Front seats were (and remain) both comfortable and supportive. Backrests recline and flip-up headrests support the neck. Lacking the forward engine of the World Car, the rear seats were too upright for excursions into dreamland, but how often were these 406s, more a personal than a business car, going to transport rear passengers. There are headrests of a sort but wrongly positioned for the neck. Their other purpose is to protect against the very solid unyielding metal catches which have to be rigid to keep the rear windows open at cruising speeds.

Wireless and other extras were fitted as ordered. Bristol Cars still had the facilities for protecting, painting and furnishing the bodies. A galaxy of attractive colours, even more than before, were offered in the brochure (note this was issued by Bristol Siddeley Engines Ltd in October 1959 during that short period in which they were in control), which in their words 'enhances the 406's inherent distinction by making possible a wide variety of individual combinations'. Colours available were Bristol Red, Dark Green, Black, Sable, Light Beige, three Greys and both Midnight and Pastel Blue. The paints could be used singly or in two tone. Records show that the various greys were most popular. There were just six black cars. Leather upholstery was available in seven different shades and there was a colour choice for the carpets. Few, if any, identical cars were despatched. Despite all this enormous care for detail, neither at Jones Brothers nor at Filton did they find the long-term solution to preventing corrosion at the edges of the wheel arches. A compound known as Duralac, designed to inhibit electrolytic decomposition between dissimilar metals, which they inserted between the steel and aluminium, staves off the problem, as does restoration of blemished paint. After many years metal may have to be replaced.

At Filton the cars were fitted with the best available cross-ply tyres for which the suspension was designed. In later years cross-plies were still recommended by Eric Storey. The author has frequently crossed Europe on those perfectly surfaced autoroutes as it were skimming the tarmac on those cross-plies. It is a unique sensation. Such is the stability that it is almost as if flying above the surface of the road – and always that lovely fresh air with the windows open. This octogenarian has frequently been reluctant to stop on the run down from Caen to Toulouse or Calais to Perpignan. However on the now appalling UK road surfaces some may prefer the flexing of modern radials to put comfort before stability. That evocatively written 406 brochure, perhaps from G. W.'s pen, tells all: 'The very high performance of the Type 406 saloon is perhaps the least of its virtues. Its elegance and comfort tend to disguise its ability to cover long distances in astonishingly short times with the minimum of fatigue for driver and passengers. The overdrive fifth gear permits a high cruising speed at moderate engine speed and, since the clean aerodynamic form of the body reduces wind noise as well as wind resistance, the Bristol 406 achieves an unusual standard of ease and silence at high speeds.' How true these words are. So often I have reached the end of a journey and thought: 'How can I have got here already?' It's those comfortable seats and the driving position, the vision out from the close to the eyes screen, that ventilation. The controls are precise and well weighted, there is no sway or lurch or irritating vibration. And, because of the existence of knowledgeable workshops who specialise in maintaining these cars, they can be kept in good order. Looked after they can last a very long time.

As with many human creations, the 406 is not without fault. Much low-gear travel is necessary to enable that just 2.2-litre engine to propel that large saloon up Alpine or Pyrenean passes. Looking back, almost all the Bristol-engined cars were deficient in some respect: the 400 with lack of space and small windows, 401 and 403 could be tail heavy with full load, 404 and 405 that wood construction, 406 as above. These were not matters of concern with low production numbers. They were part of progress towards the faultless World Car; however, along the way Filton did create a masterpiece, a special shorter 406S on an extension of the 404 body buck. After a vast mileage owned by a vet in Scotland, it has been diligently rebuilt in recent years and remains in the safe hands of a knowledgeable and caring owner. It is a superb creation. Anthony Crook sent another short chassis 406 to Zagato in Milan. It was on display with a most attractive body at Earl's Court in 1960 and it too is watched over by an owner with understanding. Six other full-length chassis went to Milan. Zagato's lighter-weight body was nearly a foot shorter; also lower and with less garnish. These also remain attractive and valuable specimens.

Author's current 406 in original colour – Andorra.

Above: 406. Sorteney, Andorra.

Below: Author's 406 after colour change. With 401, 1996 FIVA Rally, UK.

Above: In between 406 Zagato and 404. Le Mans.

Below: 2019 FIVA Rally Andorra. Bristol V8 603 other side of Mercedes.

Above: Harry Wareham, then Owner's Club chairman, with short-chassis 406 Zagato.

Below: Bristol's own short-chassis 406 after renovation at Filton.

Bristol 406 Zagato on display at Earl's Court.

It is also known that Zagato re-bodied a few 400s in a similar style. There is particular personal memory of one car retired to Devon having travelled a prodigious mileage along the Libyan coast road driven by its oil surveyor owner. Evocative as I too travelled that road during Army 'National Service' in the early 1950s – deserted, straight as an arrow till you came to some S bends near the sea. No speed limits. How the owner must have enjoyed that car. There is also the one chassis ordered by and bodied by Beutler, the car we saw at the Chardonnet Service Station in 1964.

Another achievement of the 1950s already mentioned was the number of power units which Bristol Engines continued to build for sale after the AFN contract. This was another example of G. W.'s shrewd thinking. Presumably Bristol Cars, who had obtained the business, kept some of the money before making payment to Bristol Engines. In all, 816 separate engines were built, eighty-two already sent to AFN and now 695 for AC, leaving thirty-nine built for other companies or individuals. The engine had proved itself in the 450. In 1957 an AC Bristol was tenth at Le Mans, in 1958 8th and 9th and in 1959 7th. Engines had also been sold to other companies like A. Crook Motors, Cooper, E. R. A., H. R. G., Joe Kelly, Cyril Keift and Brian Lister, also to individuals like M. Anthony, J. W. E. Banks, Jack Brabham, Cliff Davis, Hans Osterman in Sweden and Ronnie Parkinson. An appendix gives the numbers for the different types of engines. Prices varied between £400 and £500. Then there was also the contract with Freeman Marine for twenty-seven Marine gearboxes. It is also clear that they took on work

Working at Filton.

Completed 406s at Filton on bodies returned from Jones Brothers.

One of Bristol Cars' own publicity photographs of 406.

requested by Bristol Aeroplane or were prepared to take on other tasks. The separate Bristol Cars remained an active Company with G. W. taking every opportunity which would help to maintain the car side.

The thought returns that, if G. W. had been able to 'escape' earlier, or if his shareholding in Bristol Aeroplane had been equivalent to (or even larger than R. V-S.), as it might have been with different inheritance taxation, this could have been a very different story. But also, as things were, and with the enormous difficulties which he had to face, R. V-S.'s courageous decisions are to be admired. This is a tale of gritty human experience. G. W. was near to an achievement which could have given Britain a world-beating car industry today. This is the tale which needs to be better known. As it was, when there were those delays with the 3.6-litre engine, they were casting around for alternatives. James Watt had noted the V8 Chrysler on his visits to Arnolt and brought back some plans to Filton. In his letters Ken Oakes told me G. W. asked him to investigate the possibility of fitting such an engine into the 405 chassis whilst retaining its front suspension. Ken wrote: 'the problem was to get it in between the converging chassis side rails and the front cross-member. The only solution seemed to be to extend the chassis and wheelbase about eight inches and make a new oil pan to sit above the cross-member. No one seemed enthusiastic about this modification at that stage.'

The subsequent development of the V8 under the direction and management of Anthony Crook is a different story which includes some of the other people who had been involved at Filton and remained for the V8 era. There are people like wiring loom wizard Syd Lovesy, who would take charge of V8 production but had been with Bristol since the beginning; Syd Gibbens with his formidable knowledge of all parts; Jeff Marsh, also good with wiring who became workshop manager and much else; Eden Holder and Eric Ager, both dedicated technicians; and Mrs Hurkett with her encyclopaedic knowledge in the office. I also hope, if such a book is undertaken, it will record how cruel fate later prevented G. W., appreciated by all those who worked with him, from receiving the recognition he truly deserves. Learning that I was working on this book, a former Bristol Cars employee, who does not want to be named, has just recently sent handwritten record books which he rescued some years ago. The table in Appendix 1 shows the number of six-cylinder cars exported in the seven years between 1949 and 1955. This confirms the earlier comment that knowledge, experience and reputation of the Bristol car had been built up throughout the world. These figures should tie up with the information on the sales cards recently reproduced in the Palawan book *The Car Division*. They will be more easily accessible here.

406 chassis with body designed and built by Beutler in Switzerland.

Above: 406 without engine (taken for circuit racing cars) retrieved from Northern Ireland.

Below: Corrosion if not looked after correctly.

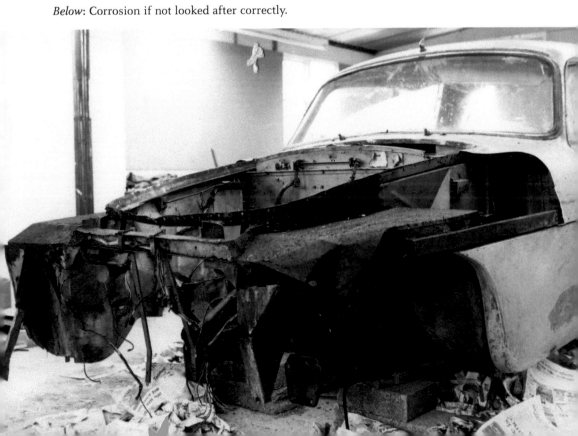

Above: 404, 406, 405 drophead and saloon in front of Britannia.

Below: AC Ace and Frazer Nash Sebring both with six-cylinder Bristol engines.

405 parked before Volcan Villarrica, Chile.

Had other events not prevented this fine car being produced in a new Filton factory, it seems a fair assumption that the project would have moved into profit. This would have amply justified G. W.'s predictions and hopes for the World Car and eased the acceptance of earlier losses. More than that. What if the cars were already being built in a separate factory established in the 1960s on a separate site and with other family or associated management in place at the time of G. W.'s accident? Then, when the ownership of the Filton aeroplane factory and airfield were taken over by the government from April 1977 until full privatisation again in 1985, could this other factory have remained with the founding family? It is yet another reminder of Fritz Feidler's warning about having car and aeroplane production on the same site. It is also another example of the vision of a brilliant British engineer and entrepreneur being destroyed by events and actions outside of their control.

Export Destinations

Country	1947	1948	1949	1950	1951	1952	1953	1954	1955
Argentina	1 x 400		1 x 400						
Australia		25 x 400	3 x 401 34 x 400 3 x 402	21 x 400 4 x 401	52 x 401	1 x 401	3 x 401 14 x 403	3 x 404	7 x 405 2 x 404
Austria			1 x 400	1 x 400					
Belgium		2 x 400	2 x 400	2 x 400		8 x 400 1 x 402	7 x 401	5 x 403 2 x 404	1 x 405
Brazil		2 x 400							
Canada				2 x 400		1 x 401			2 x 405
Ceylon					1 x 401				
Czech		2 x 400							
Egypt			1 x 400		1 x 400				
France			4 x 400	2 x 400	5 x 401	6 x 401	6 x 401 11 x 403	6 x 404	3 x 404 8 x 405
Gibraltar				1 x 401					
Holland					1 x 401	1 x 401	2 x 401	1 x 403	
Hong Kong						1 x 401			

Country								
Ireland	5 x 400	1 x 401	1 x 401	4 x 401	1 x 401 2 x 403	5 x 403	1 x 404	3 x 405
Italy	3 x 400		2 x 400					
Jersey			1 x 401	1 x 401	1 x 401	1 x 403	1 x 403	1 x 405
Jordan					1 x 401			
Kenya						1 x 401		1 x 405
Lebanon								1 x 405
Malaya							1 x 402	
Morocco		1 x 401		1 x 401	2 x 401	1 x 403	1 x 403	
New Zealand				6 x 401		1 x 403	1 x 405	1 x 405
Pakistan							1 x 403	
Portugal			1 x 401	1 x 401	1 x 401	2 x 403	1 x 404	1 x 405
S. Arabia					1 x 402			1 x 405
S. Africa	1 x 400							
S. Rhodesia					2 x 401			1 x 405
Spain			1 x 402					3 x 405
Sweden	4 x 400		1 x 400	1 x 401 1 x 402	2 x 401		1 x 403	
Switzerland*			8 x 400	8 x 401		2 x 401	1 x 404	
Tangier				2 x 401		1 x 403		
USA			1 x 401	3 x 401	4 x 401	4 x 403	2 x 404	1 x 405

*Also many chassis – see text.

These figures are collated from different sources. They may not be completely accurate but give an idea of export achievement.

APPENDIX 2

Separate Engine Sales

TYPE NUMBER	TOTAL BUILT
85C	4
100A	5
100B	38
100C	17
100D	611
110	6
BS.1	52
BS2	3
BS.4	22
FNS	57
Cooper special development	1

The total number on a list dated 30 June 1960 is given as 816.

Appendix 3

Larger Distributors

NUMBERS SOLD	400	401	402	403	404	405	406
BRADBURN WEDGE	8	18	10	6	18	8	8 (B&W)
BROUGHTON	6 (2ch)	9					
CEDAR	13	17	5	2		5 (2dh)	4
CROOK	8	35	3	32	8	33 (5dh)	25
CRUICKSHANK	7	16	2	7	1	11 (1dh)	
FUGGLE	11 (1dh)	18				11	17
GALT	20	41	1	11	3	6 (2dh)	
MARTINDALE (later Bolton)	3	20	1	9	1	18 (4dh)	12
NEWMAN	6	11	9	1		9 (2dh)	
SANDERS	12	18	7	1		4 (2dh)	
WATSON	4	16	7	1	2		
UNIVERSITY	23	83	5	48	3	31 (4dh)	

Most of these dealers were large organisations with impressive showrooms in prominent positions and efficient servicing arrangements. University, for example, would have well profited from the Bristol Association. They all saw a future in the forthcoming World Car and were fully supportive. It was so different to later years with just one London showroom in Kensington.

APPENDIX 4

Specifications of Six-cylinder Cars

400	1947–1950
Body	Close-coupled. Wood and steel. Side-opening bonnet. Two rear-hinged doors. Rear spare on boot lid (early cars inside boot).
Engine	85,85A,85B,85C. Capacity. 1,971cc.
Gearbox	Four-speed. Free-wheel first gear.
Suspension	Front. Transverse leaf. Rear. Torsion bars and A bracket. Bristol-made shock absorbers.
Steering	Rack and pinion.
Brakes	Cast-iron drum.
Wheel/tyre	5.50 x 16 cross-ply.
Recognition.	1930s appearance. Front sliding windows. Separate sweeping wings. BMW-type grille.

400 Open	1947–1948
Body	Three four-seaters. Opening roof. Two drophead, one tourer.

ONLY CHANGES GIVEN FOR SUBSEQUENT MODELS

401	1948–1953
Body	Roomier four-seater. Aluminium over steel tube. Front-hinged doors with push button entry. Front seats rake adjustment.
Engine	85C.
Suspension	From chassis 1006: Bought-in telescopic shock absorbers.
Brakes	Later button release handbrake.

Recognition	First aerodynamic body. Bristol badges yellow background. Early. Ridge along bottom of sides. Rubber bump mount. Later. No ridge. Sprung metal bumper mount.
Body	Bradburn and Wedge-backed creation of one drophead.

402	1948–1950
Body	Drophead. Two-door four-seater with opening roof.

403	1953–1955
Body	Superior heating/ventilation. Fresh or re-circulated air.
Engine	100A. Last batch 100B/B2
Suspension	Front anti-roll bar.
Brakes	Alfin alloy drum.
Wheels	5.75 x 16
Recognition	Badges red background. 403 numerals on bonnet. Last batch. Sidelights on top of wings.

404	1953–1955
Body	Two-door two-seater (occasional rear) on shorter chassis. No opening rear panel. Part wood construction.
Engine	100B or 100C.
Wheels	5.50 x 16.
Recognition	Open front air intake. Spare behind left front wheel.

405	1954–1958
Body	Four-door four/five-seater. Petrol tank above rear axle. Boot.
Engine	100 B2. Overdrive now added.
Recognition	Four side windows. Three section rear window. Bonnet air duct. Central spotlight at front.

405 drophead	1954–1956
Body	Two-door four-seater with opening roof.

406	1958–1961
Body	Two large doors. No wood in construction. Big boot.
Engine	110. Now 2216 cc
Suspension	Watt link for rear suspension.

Brakes	Disc.
Wheels	6.00 x 16.
Recognition	Two side windows. No bonnet air duct. Repeater roof indicator lights. Fog and spot lights above bumper.

406 S short chassis 1958–1959

Body	Two door. No opening boot. One Bristol body, one Zagato. Also six standard chassis for lighter bodywork by Zagato.

APPENDIX 5

Bristol Assistance

AUTOCAR REPAIRS   South London
www.@autocar-repairs.co.uk
Repair and service

JONATHAN BRADBURN   Isle of Man
www.jbradburn.co.uk
Engines, gearboxes and other parts for Bristols and ACs.

BRISTOL OWNER'S CLUB
www.boc.net
Membership Secretary. mem.sec@boc.net

BRISTOL OWNER'S AND DRIVER'S ASSOCIATION
www.bristoloda.org
Membership Secretary. memsec@bristoloda.org

BRISTOL OWNERS HERITAGE TRUST
bristolownersht.com also stefan@cembrowicz.co.uk

BRISTOL ARCHIVES
archives.bristol.gov.uk 46120
B Bond Warehouse, Smeaton Road, Bristol, BS1 6XN. Tuesdays to Fridays and first two
Saturdays of each month.

CLASSIC BRISTOL CAR PARTS CO   Hampshire
graeme.payne@cbcpc.co.uk
Bristol Parts.

COLEMAN CLASSIC CARS LTD   Berkshire
www.colemanclassiccars.co.uk
Repair, re-build and service.

HC CLASSICS   Wiltshire
www.hcclassics.co.uk
vehicle upholstery, sound systems.

LONGSTONE CLASSIC TYRES   Derbyshire
www.longstone.com
Tyres and tyre advice.

MITCHELL MOTORS RESTORATION LTD   Wiltshire
www.mitchellmotors.co.uk
Bodywork, painting, full restoration.

OLIVER PENNEY ENGINEERING   Oxfordshire
www.oliverpenney.com
Engine and gearbox.

ONE-TO-ONE TRIMMERS   Kent
www.one-to-onetrimmers.co.uk

IAN NUTHALL Ltd   Nottingham
www.inracing.co.uk
Repairs, race and rally preparation

CHARLES RUSSELL   Wiltshire
Repair, restoration and service.
vsc_engineers@lineone.net

SLJ HACKETT   Wiltshire
www.sljhackett.co.uk
Bristol sales.

SPENCER LANE-JONES LTD   Wiltshire
www.spencer-lj.com
Repair, restoration and service.

JIM STOKES WORKSHOPS GROUP   Hampshire
www.triplembyjswl.com

Further Reading

Balfour, C., *Bristol Cars: A Very British Story* (Haynes, 2009)

Banks, Air Commodore F. R., *I Kept No Diary* (Airlife, 1978)

Barnes, C. H., Bristol Aircraft Since 1910 (Putnam, 1964)

Bristol Owner's Heritage Trust, *Bristol Car Division* (Palawan, 2018)

Gibb, Walter, *Filton Voices* (Tempus, 2003)

Gunston, Bill, *By Jupiter: The Life of Sir Roy Fedden* (Royal Aeronautical Society, 1978)

Hooker, Sir Stanley, *Not Much of An Engineer* (Airlife, 1984)

Jenkinson, D., *Chain Drive to Turbocharger* (Patrick Stephens, 1984)

Jennings, R. L., *Frazer Nash: What Memories That Name Arouses*!

Lovesey, Syd, *Filton Voices* (Tempus Publishing, 2003)

Oxley, Charles, *The Quiet Survivor* (Oxley-Sidey, 1988)

Palmer, Michael, *Bristol Cars Model by Model* (Crowood Press, 2015)

Setright, L. J. K., *A Private Car* (Palawan Press, 1998)

Smith, Bill, *Armstrong Siddeley Motors* (Veloce, 2006)

Trigwell, James and Pritchard Anthony, *Post-War Fraser Nash* (Palawan)

Wall, Sir Robert, *Bristol Aircraft* (Halsgrove, 2000)

White, Sir George, *Tramlines to the Stars* (Redcliffe Press, 1995)

Acknowledgements

Our special thanks are due to three people who have done so much to help by diligently reading through the text and making suggestions about this book. First, Sir George White, son of G. W. and great-grandson of the first Sir George, who has himself done so much to record the enormous achievements of his family in the wider transport arena. Second, Spencer Lane-Jones who, after twenty-seven years' service in the Royal Engineers, retired as a Lieutenant-Colonel and in 1987 established Spencer Lane-Jones Ltd, now known as SLJ and until recently managed by Peter Campbell. This company has gained worldwide renown for the restoration, repair and servicing of both six-cylinder and V-engined Bristol cars. Third, Dr Stefan Cembrowicz, who has led the establishment of The Bristol Owner's Heritage Trust preserving documents and photographs, now in partnership with The Bristol City Archives in Smeaton Road (archives.bristol.gov.uk46120).

It is to Lisa Waygood, and to Michael Sommer who introduced us, that we owe enormous thanks for helping us to sort out pictures received from different sources, particularly Sir George White, Geoffrey Herdman, Simon Brindle and the Heritage Trust. Time and again, with immense patience, Lisa came to our rescue when our computer skills were lacking and her own knowledge of car and racing history was invaluable. Simon Draper has kindly agreed to our using the picture of the 'World Car' chassis on test outside the Brabazon Hanger, also shown in the magnificent Palawan *Car Division* book. My wife, Ann, together with son, daughters and grandchildren, have once again been a tremendous and calming support to the whole project.

Brian Marelli, whilst working with Anthony Crook rather than at Filton, has been a source of advice and assistance with our own cars for over fifty years. Toby Silverton, who tried so hard to give Bristol Cars another lease of life, provided another valuable perspective on the earlier years. Then our thanks also to the community of knowledgeable owners and skilled technicians, especially Nick Cooper and Charles Russell, who have made Bristol ownership such a pleasurable part of our lives for so many years.